*Thanks to
Anita, Ginny, Louise, Rose , and Tita
for your friendship, guidance and inspiration.*

Special Thanks

to those who provided help from:
Franklin D. Roosevelt Presidential Library and Museum
John F. Kennedy Presidential Library and Museum
Gerald R. Ford Presidential Library and Museum
The Ronald Reagan Presidential Foundation and Library

Presidents of the United States of America

1. George Washington
2. John Adams
3. Thomas Jefferson
4. James Madison
5. James Monroe
6. John Quincy Adams
7. Andrew Jackson
8. Martin Van Buren
9. William Henry Harrison
10. John Tyler
11. James K. Polk
12. Zachary Taylor
13. Millard Fillmore
14. Franklin Pierce
15. James Buchanan
16. Abraham Lincoln
17. Andrew Johnson
18. Ulysses S. Grant
19. Rutherford B. Hayes
20. James A. Garfield
21. Chester A. Arthur
22. Grover Cleveland
23. Benjamin Harrison
24. Grover Cleveland
25. William McKinley
26. Theodore Roosevelt
27. William Howard Taft
28. Woodrow Wilson
29. Warren G. Harding
30. Calvin Coolidge
31. Herbert Hoover
32. Franklin D. Roosevelt
33. Harry S. Truman
34. Dwight D. Eisenhower
35. John F. Kennedy
36. Lyndon B. Johnson
37. Richard M. Nixon
38. Gerald R. Ford
39. James Carter
40. Ronald Wilson Reagan
41. George H. W. Bush
42. William J. Clinton
43. George W. Bush
44. Barack H. Obama

Illustrations copyright © 2012 Susan Castriota

Manuscript copyright © 2012 Susan Castriota

Book copyright © 2012 Susan Castriota, Upper St. Clair, PA

Written and Illustrated by Susan Castriota

Cover and Book Design: Faye Klein

Second Edition 2012

www.wilsongetsadopted.com

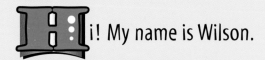**i**! My name is Wilson.

I thought I was a lucky dog until I learned about the Presidents' dogs. Many of them lived in the White House. Yes — I am talking about THE White House. The home where the U. S. Presidents and their families have lived for more than 200 years!

You can imagine how many other pets have also lived in the White House. There were ponies, birds, cats, goats, cows, and even a raccoon! Since I am a dog, I am going to visit the very famous White House Pups!

Welcome to 1600 Pennsylvania Avenue.

George Washington (1789-1797) was our first President. He did not live at the White House. It had not been built yet. He had many "first dogs" and brought us a new breed. This breed is called the American foxhound.

John Adams (1797-1801) had two mixed-breed dogs named Juno and Satan.

Thomas Jefferson (1801-1809) had many briard breed dogs. One of the dogs was named Buzzy. Jefferson wrote the first dog license law in Virginia.

Buzzy

"Rover, you were the first dog of the first President!"

James Monroe (1817-1825) had many pets. His dog was a spaniel named Buddy. He was a gift from the French General Lafayette.

John Tyler (1841-1845) had three dogs. Two were Irish wolfhounds and one Italian greyhound. LeBeau, the greyhound, was a gift to the First Lady.

Franklin Pierce (1853-1857) was given a tiny "sleeve dog" from Japan, small enough to fit into a tea cup.

James Buchanan (1857-1861) had many pets. Lara, a Newfoundland breed, was the largest White House dog. She weighed 170 pounds.

Abraham Lincoln (1861-1865) had Fido, a mixed-breed dog. Fido was the first President's dog to have his picture taken in a portrait studio.

Ulysses S. Grant (1869-1877) had a Newfoundland dog named Faithful and a dog named Rosie.

Rutherford B. Hayes (1877-1881) had many dogs. Grimm was his beloved greyhound. The whole country was sad when Grimm died.

James A. Garfield (1881-1881) had a mixed-breed dog named Veto.

Grimm

"Fido, say biscuit and smile!"

Grover Cleveland (1885-1889 & 1893-1897) had a poodle ... just like me!

Benjamin Harrison (1889-1893) had many pets. One was a collie mix dog named Dash.

Theodore Roosevelt (1901-1909) had many pets. His daughter Alice had Manchu, a black Pekingese dog. Manchu was a gift from the Empress of China. The President called his many mixed-breeds "Heinz pickle" dogs.

William H. Taft (1909-1913) had a dog named Caruso. The dog was a gift to his daughter Helen from the opera singer Enrico Caruso.

Dash

"Manchu, why don't you make room for Pete up here with us?"

Warren G. Harding (1921-1923) had Old Boy, an English bulldog. Laddie Boy, the famous Airedale dog, had his own chair to sit on in meetings. Dogs were invited to the White House for his birthday party!

Calvin Coolidge (1923-1929) had many pets. Rob Roy, the white collie dog, loved the First Lady. She chose him to be painted with her in a White House portrait.

Herbert Hoover (1929-1933) had many dogs. King Tut, was a Belgian shepherd. He was a patrol dog for the White House police force.

Rob Roy

"Yumm, biscuit birthday cake, can't wait!"

Franklin D. Roosevelt (1933-1945) had many dogs. The most famous was Fala. He was a little black Scottish terrier. As the star of two MGM films, he received many letters from fans. Fala is the only dog statue to join his master at a national monument.

Harry S. Truman (1945-1953) had two dogs. Feller was a cocker spaniel and Mike was an Irish setter. President Truman said, "If you want to have a friend in Washington, you should buy a dog."

Dwight D. Eisenhower (1953-1961) had Heidi, a weimaraner.

Heidi

Out for a joy ride with Fala.
Beep beep!

John F. Kennedy (1961-1963) had many pets. His daughter Caroline was given Pushinka, a mixed-breed dog from the Soviet Premier. She was the pup of Strelka, one of the first dogs in space. Pushinka and Charlie, a Welsh terrier, had four puppies. President Kennedy referred to them as "Pupniks"!

Lyndon B. Johnson (1963-1969) had many dogs. His beagles were named Him and Her. They appeared on the cover of <u>LIFE</u> magazine. Yuki was a mixed-breed dog. Yuki appeared on the front page of a newspaper for biting a White House policeman!

Him and Her

Dog in space, "pupniks" on the ground!

Richard M. Nixon (1969-1974) had three dogs. Vicky was a poodle, Pasha, a terrier, and King Timahoe was an Irish setter. The dogs were famous for their Christmas card photos.

Gerald Ford (1974-1977) had two golden retriever dogs. Liberty, the mom, gave birth to eight puppies at the White House. One pup named Misty stayed as a pet. A pup named Gerry was donated to the Leader Dogs for the Blind school. Gerry was trained to be a guide dog.

Jimmy Carter (1977-1981) had a Border collie dog named Grits.

Vicky   Pasha

Liberty is so proud of her guide dog pup.

Ronald Reagan (1981-1989) had many dogs Lucky was a Bouvier des Flandres, and Rex was a Cavalier King Charles. Rex had a dog house that looked like the White House. Rex's first duty was to help light the national Christmas tree.

George H. W. Bush (1989-1993) had two English springer spaniel dogs. Millie was the mom, and Ranger was one of her pups. Millie was the author of a dog book. The book was a big hit and raised money for charities.

Millie

William J. Clinton (1993-2001) had a brown Labrador retriever dog named Buddy. The First Lady wrote a book about Buddy and Socks the cat. The book raised money for charities.

George W. Bush (2001-2009) had three dogs. Two were black Scottish terriers named Barney and Miss Beazley. Miss Beazley was a birthday gift to the First Lady. Her nickname was "Beazley Weazley." Barney became the first White House dog to become a webcam star. He wandered through the White House with a video camera on his collar!

Buddy

"Lights, camera, action! Miss Beazley and Barney ... take two."

Barack Obama (2009-Incumbent) has a black and white Portuguese water dog named Bo. He was a gift from Senator Ted Kennedy. The family lovingly calls Bo "America's Commander-in-Leash." Bo often joins Santa Claus to visit with children in the hospital.

I hope you enjoyed my visit with the White House Pups. As you can see, the four-legged family members also were important in our nation's history. Man's best friend has roamed the halls of the White House for more than 200 years. I am sure they will be there for many years to come!

"Hey, Bo! Since we're both water dogs, how about a dip in the fountain?"

Sweet Dreams